P9-AQL-977

HEADLINES FROM HISTORY™

George Washington Elected

How America's First President Was Chosen

Allison Stark Draper

The Rosen Publishing Group's
PowerKids Press™
New York

Hear Ye! Hear Ye! Hear Ye! Hear Ye! Hear Ye! Hear Ye! Hear Ye! Hear Ye! Hear Ye! Hear Ye! Hear

Hear Ye! Hear Ye! Hear Ye! Hear Ye! Hear Ye! Hear Ye! Hear Ye! Hear Ye!

Published in 2001 by The Rosen Publishing Group, Inc.
29 East 21st Street, New York, NY 10010

First Edition

Book Design: Michael de Guzman

Photo Credits: pp. 4, 7, 8, 11, 13, 14, 18 © North Wind Pictures; pp. 17, 21 © Bettmann/CORBIS.

Draper, Allison Stark.
George Washington elected : how America's first president was chosen / by Allison Stark Draper.
p. cm.— (Headlines from history)
Includes index.
Summary: Briefly describes George Washington's role in the American Revolution and his tenure as the first United States president.
ISBN 0-8239-5675-X (alk. paper)
1. Washington, George, 1732-1799—Juvenile literature. 2. Presidents—United States—Election—1789—Juvenile literature. 3. United States—Politics and government—1783-1809—Juvenile literature. [1. Washington, George, 1732-1799. 2. Presidents.] I. Title. II. Series.

E312.66.D7 2000 00-026176
973.4'1'092—dc21

Manufactured in the United States of America

Hear Ye! Hear Ye! Hear Ye! Hear Ye! Hear Ye! Hear Ye! Hear Ye! Hear Ye! Hear Ye! Hear

CONTENTS

George Washington Joins British in French and Indian War

Beginning in the 1600s, men and women started moving to America from England. One of England's American **colonies** was called Virginia. George Washington was born in Virginia on February 22, 1732.

In 1752, Washington joined the British army that was in America. He fought

on the side of the British with his fellow **colonists**. They were fighting a land war against the French. This war was called the French and Indian War. The war was called this because several Native American tribes helped the French fight the British. The British also had Native Americans fighting on their side. The French army had more Native Americans helping them, however.

Washington did not like the way the colonists in the British army were treated. The colonists were not paid as much money as the British soldiers. They also were not given as high a rank in the army.

George Washington fought on the side of the British during the French and Indian War. He did not think the British treated the colonial soldiers fairly, though.

George Washington Is Put in Charge of Colonial Army

Washington returned to Virginia in 1758. In 1759, he married a widow named Martha Custis. Washington became involved in the local government. He talked to colonists throughout Virginia. Many thought that the British were treating them unfairly. The colonists were British **citizens**, but they had fewer rights than people living in England did. Washington was not happy with the British, but he did not think war was the answer. He hoped that a peaceful solution could be worked out.

Washington refused to be paid for leading the colonial army. His only concern was making sure America was free from British rule.

In 1775, there was a meeting of colonial leaders, called the Second Continental **Congress**. At this meeting, Congress approved the **Declaration of Independence**. The Declaration of Independence said that the colonists should be free from British rule. When it was clear that the British and the American colonists were going to war, Washington agreed to lead the colonial troops.

Hear Ye! Hear Ye! Hear Ye! Hear Ye! Hear Ye! Hear Ye! Hear Ye! Hear Ye! Hear Ye! Hear Ye! Hear

Hear Ye! Hear Ye! Hear Ye! Hear Ye! Hear Ye! Hear Ye! Hear Ye! Hear Ye! Hear Ye! Hear Ye! Hear Ye! Hear Ye!

George Washington Leads Colonial Army to Victory

Hear Ye! Hear Ye! Hear Ye! Hear Ye! Hear Ye! Hear Ye! Hear Ye! Hear Ye! Hear Ye! Hear

The war between England and America was called the Revolutionary War. On July 3, 1775, George Washington took command of the colonial army. There were about 20,000 men in the army. Washington was a smart and brave leader. Conditions in the army were bad. There was little food and hardly any money to pay the soldiers. Many soldiers only stayed in the army because they believed in General Washington.

With Washington in charge of the army, the colonists won the war. A **treaty** ending the war was signed in Paris on September 3, 1783. On December 24, Washington returned to his house in Virginia. Washington's house was called Mount Vernon.

After the war, Washington went home to Mount Vernon to spend time with his family. He also raised dogs and horses, and grew crops.

Americans Elect George Washington As First President

In 1787, Congress asked Washington to come to Pennsylvania. The members of Congress wanted his help writing the nation's **Constitution**. After the Revolutionary War, the colonies became known as states. Each state had its own constitution. Washington knew that to be **united**, the 13 states had to have a single government with one constitution. Washington helped convince Americans in every state that the Constitution was in the country's best interest. It was during this time that the country became known as the United

Fifty-five men came to Philadelphia to work on the Constitution. Washington was tired from the war, but he believed in serving his country.

States of America.

The Americans voted for their first president in 1789. **Electors** in each state met to vote. They sent their **ballots** to Congress. The ballots were opened and counted. Every elector in every state had chosen Washington as president.

President Washington Travels Throughout the Country

After working on the Constitution, Washington returned to Mount Vernon. He was elected president and left for New York on April 16, 1789. The United States government was located in New York at that time. Washington's trip to New York was like a parade. He met citizens, government officials, and soldiers in every town. The people rang church bells. The soldiers fired guns. On April 30, 1789, Washington was sworn into office in New York City.

Washington wanted the newly formed United States to be

New York City was the center of the U.S. government in 1789. Now the center is in Washington, D.C.

a strong country. He did not want the United States to depend on Europe for food or other goods. In 1789, Washington traveled to the northern states. In 1791, he traveled to the southern states. As president, Washington wanted every state to feel like an important part of the new country.

George Washington Begins His Presidency

President Washington knew that he needed wise men around him to help run the government. He brought together a team of men to help him make decisions. Washington put John Jay in charge of the courts. He put Alexander Hamilton in charge of the government's money. He

made Thomas Jefferson the **secretary of state**. The secretary of state handles the government's dealings with other countries.

Washington worried about war. He believed that a country always needed to be ready to defend itself. Washington also wanted to make sure that there was enough money to run the government. Under Washington's rule, Alexander Hamilton taxed landowners. He also taxed goods brought in from other countries. This money was used to run the government. Some of the money helped pay for the Revolutionary War.

President Washington chose wise men to help him run the government. Their advice helped get the country off to a strong start.

United States Pushes Native Americans West

In 1790, the western border of the United States went as far as Ohio. The people of Ohio often fought with the Native Americans. The Americans built farms where the Native Americans lived and hunted. They even destroyed their homes. The Americans made it impossible for the Native Americans to live and eat. The Native Americans attacked and sometimes burned the farmers' homes.

President Washington wanted to protect the people of Ohio from the Native Americans. In 1792, he sent soldiers to Ohio. The Native Americans surprised the soldiers and

General Wayne was called "Mad Anthony" because he was such a fearless leader.

won many battles against them. Washington then put General Anthony Wayne in charge of the soldiers. General Wayne's men fought hard. They won a battle against the Native Americans at a place called Fallen Timbers. After winning this battle, the United States continued to push the Native Americans farther west.

Whiskey Rebellion Put Down by President Washington

In 1794, President Washington put a tax on whiskey to help raise money for the government. Whiskey is an alcoholic drink made from grain. The tax upset grain farmers in Pennsylvania. The farmers made most of the whiskey sold

in the United States. They thought the tax on whiskey was unfair.

Many farmers refused to pay the whiskey tax. Some farmers attacked the men who came to collect the tax. In July of 1794, a tax collector's home was burned. Washington used soldiers from the states of Pennsylvania, New Jersey, and Maryland to stop the **rebellion**. In October the soldiers ended the rebellion. The farmers had to keep paying the tax. Washington proved that the government was strong enough to make Americans obey the law.

After farmers attacked tax collectors, Washington sent in soldiers to stop what was known as the Whiskey Rebellion.

President Washington Puts America First

In the late 1700s, there were still British soldiers **stationed** south of the Great Lakes. The Great Lakes are a chain of five lakes in the northern United States and in Canada. The land where the soldiers were stationed belonged to the Americans. Washington sent John Jay, the man in charge of the courts, to England to talk to the British. In 1794, the British agreed to leave the land that belonged to the United States.

At this time there was a war going on in France. The war was between France and England. Secretary of State Jefferson wanted the United States to help the French.

President Washington did not want to get involved in another country's war. He believed that it was best for America not to take sides when it came to wars being fought outside its borders.

With John Jay's help, America and England found a peaceful solution to their problems. In 1794 the two countries signed the Jay Treaty, which was named after John Jay.

President Washington Returns to Mount Vernon

George Washington left office in 1797. He had been president for eight years. The United States government was working well. Americans wanted Washington to stay in office, but he refused. He went home to his family in Virginia. John Adams, who had been Washington's **vice president**, was elected president. Washington died at Mount Vernon on December 14, 1799. He was 67 years old.

Washington was a brave soldier and a strong leader. He loved his country and gave his time and energy to help it become a powerful nation. There were many men and women who helped make America great, but Washington will always be remembered as the "father of our country."

GLOSSARY

ballots (BAL-uts) Pieces of paper used in voting.

citizens (SIH-tih-zenz) People who are born or have the legal right to live in a country.

colonies (KAH-luh-neez) Areas in a new country where a large group of people move, who are still ruled by the leaders and laws of their old country.

colonists (KAH-luh-nists) People who live in a colony.

Congress (KON-gres) The part of the United States government that makes laws. The members of Congress are chosen by the people of their state.

constitution (kahn-stih-TOO-shun) The basic rules by which a state or country is run.

Declaration of Independence (deh-kluh-RAY-shun UV in-duh-PEN-dints) A paper signed on July 4, 1776, declaring that the American colonies were free from English rule.

electors (ee-LEK-torz) People who choose which candidate is put in a government office.

rebellion (re-BEL-yun) A fight against one's government.

secretary of state (SEK-ruh-ter-ee OV STAYT) The person in the government who is in charge of one country's relationship with other countries.

stationed (STAY-shund) Assigned to a certain place or job.

treaty (TREE-tee) A formal agreement, especially one between nations, signed and agreed upon by each nation.

united (yoo-NY-ted) Coming together to act as a single group.

vice president (VYS PRES-uh-dent) The person second in position to the president.

INDEX

WEB SITES

To find out more about George Washington's election to the presidency, check out these Web sites:

http://www.mountvernon.org

http://www.whitehouse.gov/WH/glimpse/presidents/html/gw1.html